A DAY IN THE LIFE OF A
Sports Therapist

by David Paige
Photography by Roger Ruhlin

Troll Associates

Library of Congress Cataloging in Publication Data

Paige, David, (date)
    A day in the life of a sports therapist.

    Summary: Follows the sports physical therapist for
a professional football team through his day as he
monitors the general health of the players, supervises
their nutritional needs, suggests exercises, and
administers therapy.
    1. Sports medicine—Vocational guidance—Juvenile
literature.   2. Physical therapy—Vocational guidance—
Juvenile literature.   3. Physical education and training—
Juvenile literature. [1. Physical therapists.
2. Sports medicine.   3. Occupations.   4. Caito, Fred]
I. Ruhlin, Roger, ill.   II. Title.
RC1210.P25   1985   613.7′1′023   84-2433
ISBN 0-8167-0099-0 (lib. bdg.)
ISBN 0-8167-0100-8 (pbk.)

The author and publisher wish to thank the Chicago Bears professional football organization,
especially trainer and sports physical therapist Fred Caito, and public relations director
Pat McCaskey, for their generous cooperation and assistance.

Fred Caito, a sports physical therapist, begins his day in his office. But much of the day will be spent on a football field. Fred is the trainer for a professional football team. It is his job to see to it that the players are in good physical condition.

Each new player is given a fitness test when he joins the team. Fred determines how each player can improve his strength and endurance. Besides working with weights, players must also do chin-ups and push-ups. Fred explains to all players that there is a right way and a wrong way to do these exercises.

Each player's health is checked carefully. Fred records height and weight in the player's file. Players also undergo a physical examination by the team doctor. The file on each player contains a complete medical history, which includes a record of injuries and treatments.

Shoulder pads are worn to help protect a player from injury. But equipment that is too tight or loose could have the reverse effect—instead of protecting the player, it could cause an injury. Fred presses down forcefully to make sure the shoulder pads fit properly.

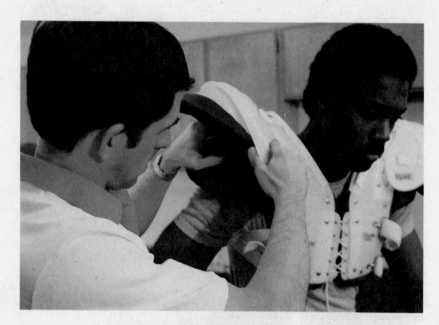

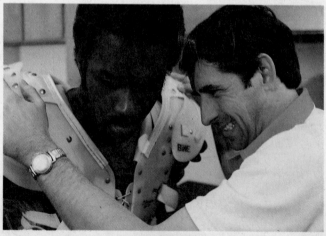

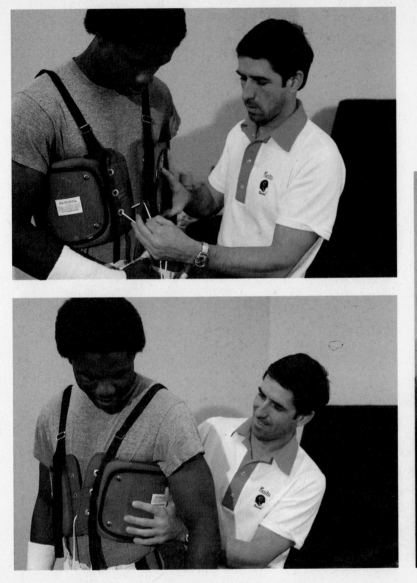

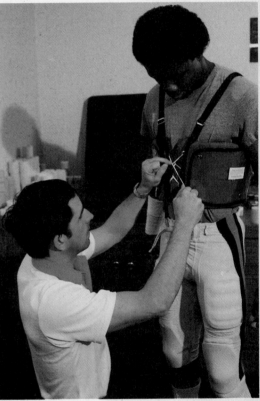

Players often need special equipment. For example, if a player has bruised ribs, he will wear a padded vest called a "flak jacket." Similar to a bulletproof vest, a flak jacket is made of a hard plastic shell that protects the ribs, plus soft padding to cushion any impact.

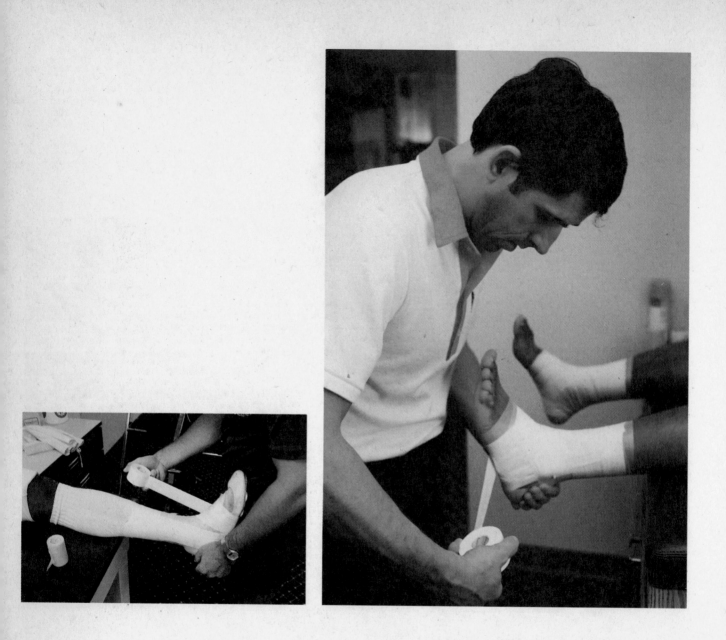

Fred and his assistants tape the ankles of all players every day before practice. This helps prevent injuries. With all the hard running and quick turns in practice or a game, it is easy for a player to sprain an ankle that is not tightly taped.

Players may also need tape on their hands, ribs, knees, or shoulders. In fact, any area of the body that is weak or injured may require the extra support provided by taping. Each day before practice Fred and his two assistants tape as many as 50 players.

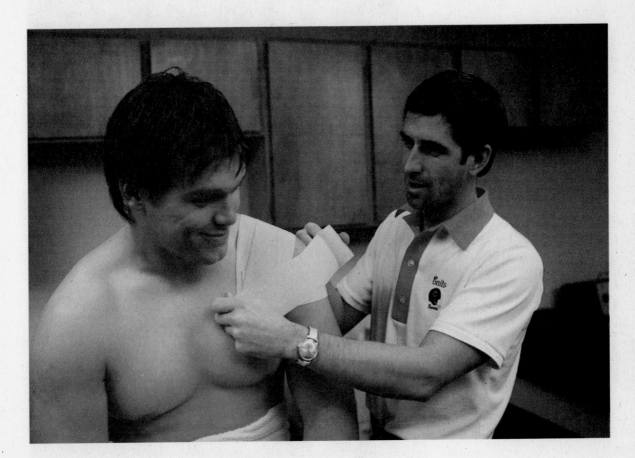

After he has finished taping the players, Fred goes out to the practice field. He talks with a player who is receiving therapy for an injured knee. Fred wants to know if the player's knee is responding to the exercises he has set up. If not, the therapy may have to be changed.

Another player complains of some tight muscles in his leg. Fred tells him to work on the hamstring —the tendon at the back of the leg. Later Fred will add this information to the player's file, along with a list of specific exercises he has recommended.

A little jogging helps the players to warm up. Then they line up for short fast races called wind sprints. Fred watches them closely. Is everyone running smoothly? After wind sprints, Fred and his assistants time each player in the 40-yard dash. This is the most basic test of a player's speed.

Next, Fred leads the players in calisthenics. These exercises are designed to make muscles flexible and strong enough to stand up to the incredible punishment of a football game. If a player is in good physical condition, he is less likely to be injured.

The players then go through a variety of rigorous drills. Each drill is aimed at developing a specific skill or strength. Blocking practice improves the skill and strength of linemen. And passing drills hone a player's ability to catch and throw a football.

A scrimmage follows calisthenics and drills. The players work on formations and plays. Or they may play a game, pitting the offense against the defense. The scrimmage is as rough as an actual game—the players hold nothing back. And Fred is there at the sidelines in the event a player gets hurt.

Both before and after the scrimmage, Fred talks to players who have been injured. Sometimes injured players are still able to practice—but Fred must keep them from overdoing it. A professional football team can't afford to lose valuable players on the practice field.

Many things can happen to a player in a football game or in practice. Fred must constantly check on the progress of the injured players. He stops on the sidelines to examine a player who was poked in the eye. If the injury seems serious, he will send the player to the team doctor for additional treatment.

Fred reports daily to the head coach. They often talk on the sidelines during a scrimmage, and they always meet at the end of the day. The coach is kept informed of the status of all injuries. Fred and his two assistants always compare notes before making a report.

Slight injuries rarely need a doctor's attention. Fred treats bumps, bruises, muscle pulls, sprained ankles, dislocated fingers, and cuts—either on the field or back in the training room. No injury is too small for treatment, not even a jammed pinky finger. These minor injuries can affect a player's ability to concentrate during practice or a game.

Fred also supervises the team's food service. Throughout the playing season, meals are prepared and served every day. Fred plans the menu with a nutrition specialist called a dietician. Football players need high-protein and high-energy foods. They work hard physically, so proper diet is important.

Fred checks the quality as well as the quantity of
the food served at every meal. He keeps records
on each player with special nutritional needs. Someone who needs to take weight off will be on a lower
calorie diet. Someone else may need to put weight
on. Fred makes sure that each player follows his
diet.

After lunch, Fred checks in on some of the players working out in the weight-training room. Using various special machines, they strengthen muscles in different parts of their bodies. An offensive lineman might build up the muscles in his arms and upper body. Other players might focus on the muscles in the back, neck, shoulders, or legs.

The weight-training room has many facilities, and each player is given "strength goals" that he is expected to meet and maintain. The competition among players for spots on the team is fierce, and strength is one of the most important factors that the coaches consider when they determine a player's value.

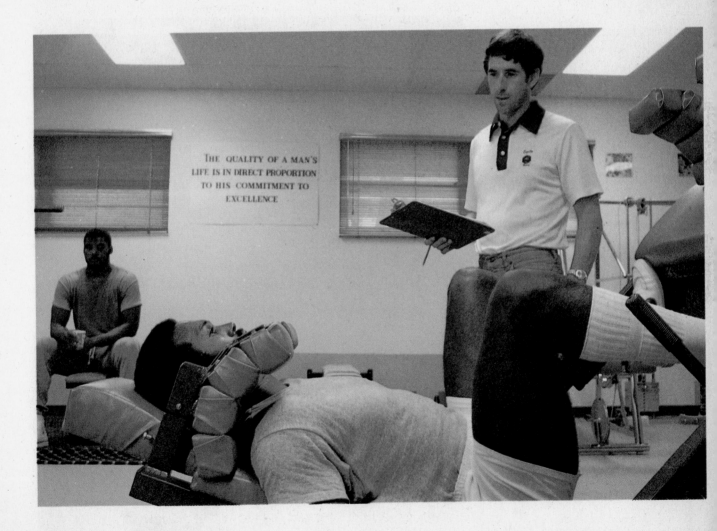

The most common major injuries suffered by football players involve the knees. A badly injured knee may take up to a year of treatment and rehabilitation before the player can return to action. Fred oversees the rehabilitation program prescribed by the doctor. He administers physical therapy to help the player gradually regain movement and strength.

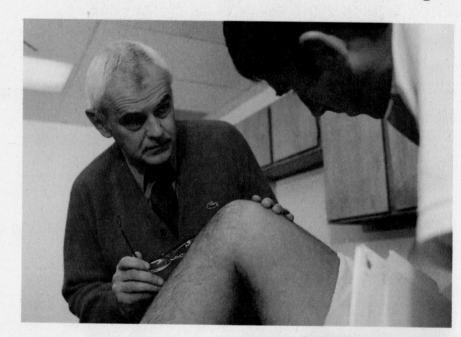

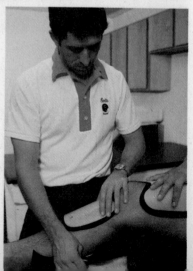

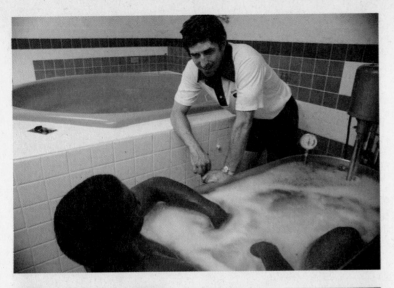

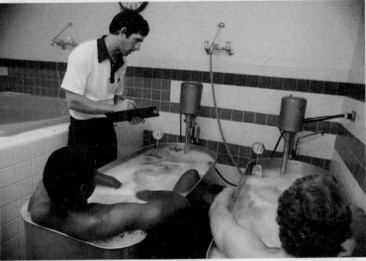

Whirlpool baths are a big help to players with sore or damaged muscles. The whirlpool provides both warmth and a water massage. Pulsing warm water relaxes injured muscles and also increases blood flow. So players begin to feel better, and their muscles heal faster.

When the team comes onto the field for the after-noon practice session, Fred must again be alert for injuries. He must be constantly ready to help newly injured players off the field and to determine how serious each injury is. Sometimes a player can "walk it off"—but sometimes special treatment is needed.

Fred does not just tell the players what to do. He often shows them exactly how to do it best. That means a lot of hard work—for Fred and for the players. But all the work is aimed at one goal—to prepare the players for the rough and rugged game they will play.

On game day, after the players have been taped, Fred takes his place on the sidelines. During the warm-up, he watches to see how the players who are returning from injuries are doing. Even when an injury has healed, if a player's muscles are not loose enough he may have to be kept out of the game until next week.

Once the game starts, it is a very busy time. Some taping here. A bruised arm there. A bloody nose. But most difficult is the decision about whether or not it is safe for an injured player to return to the game. The wrong decision could lead to an even more serious injury.

Fred and his assistants also spend a lot of time helping players recover from fatigue and from jarring hits. Both of these can dull a player's awareness, at the risk of serious injury. Often, a player who has been stunned needs a few minutes and some encouragement to recover.

After the game, Fred reviews the new injuries. He must be ready to tell the head coach who can and cannot play next week. He will work late tonight. And tomorrow, the challenging part of his work will begin anew—providing the physical therapy that will get the injured players back in shape again for next Sunday's game.

Fred is proud of the careers he has helped save and the games he has helped win simply by doing his job. The work of a sports therapist is done on the sidelines and behind the scenes, but it is vital to the success of the team. It's rewarding and it's challenging—and that's what makes it all worthwhile.